MARRIED TO A COMPUTER

Written By:
Herbert Kavet

Illustrated By:
Martin Riskin

Manufactured in the United States of America

30 29 28 27 26 25 24 23 22 21 20 19 18 17 16 15 14 13 12 11 10 9 8 7 6 5 4 3 2 1

Ivory Tower Publishing Co., Inc.
125 Walnut St., P.O. Box 9132, Watertown, MA 02272-9132
Telephone #: (617) 923-1111   Fax #: (617) 923-8839

ABOUT THE AUTHOR

The author, (that's me), when at college in 1906, once programmed an abacus in machine language—whatever that is. Perhaps it's a disgrace to M.I.T., but I've assiduously avoided computers ever since, sort of hoping they'd quietly go away. I even prefer to have my kids program the VCR. Embarrassing as it is, I have to dig out the instruction book to turn my wrist watch back or ahead with daylight savings time.

It was only the promise of fame and great financial gain that induced me to write this book, and any errors or omissions are surely my son Gregg's responsibility since I stole most of this material from him.

HOW TO TELL IF YOU ARE MARRIED TO A COMPUTER

1. You take it for granted.
2. You fondle it daily.
3. You eat most meals with it.
4. You keep in touch when you're traveling.
5. You stare at it a lot without understanding it.
6. You can't fall asleep at night unless you're cradling it in your arms.

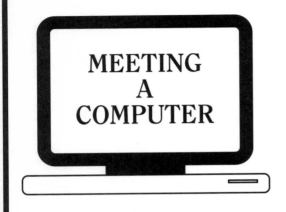

MEETING A COMPUTER

Most people who marry a computer are first introduced by a friend. Everyone has at least one friend who is a computer expert and this "friend" will try to get you to marry a computer similar to the one he or she married. This is probably a good idea since this will be the only computer they understand and can help you with. One way to meet a computer is to go into a dark closet in the most remote corner of your basement and whisper, "I think I need a computer." By the time you return to your living room, at least four friends will have appeared, each an expert on some phase of computer operations, totally different from what you are trying to accomplish, and full of conflicting advice on which machine to buy.

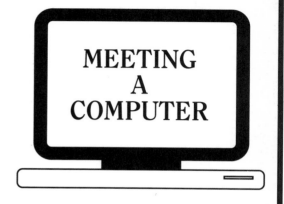

MEETING
A
COMPUTER

If you don't have any friends, don't sweat it. You can go to a computer store where a smiling salesman, often only 14 years old, will become your best friend if you have a valid Visa or Mastercharge Card in your wallet. The salesman (there are few saleswomen because they've all gotten better paying jobs with real companies) knows that once he becomes your friend he will be able to make his next 2 or 3 mortgage payments or maybe buy a new BMW. He will probably remain your friend until you call the third time for some sort of help, at which point he will be at a meeting for the rest of the day.

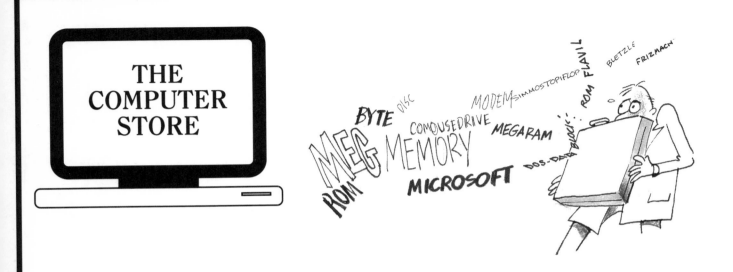

THE COMPUTER STORE

Entering a computer store is like entering a psychological boxing ring with a professional fighter. First the customer and salesperson probe and test each other. "May I help you?" "Oh, just looking. Do you have anything that can work with a Garfinkle analysis?" Then the competition begins when the salesperson and customer close with each other and start throwing around acronyms that bounce back and forth with increasing fury: "SIMMSOPTIPLOPS," "DOS DATA BLOCK," "COMOUSEDRIV," "FLAVIL."

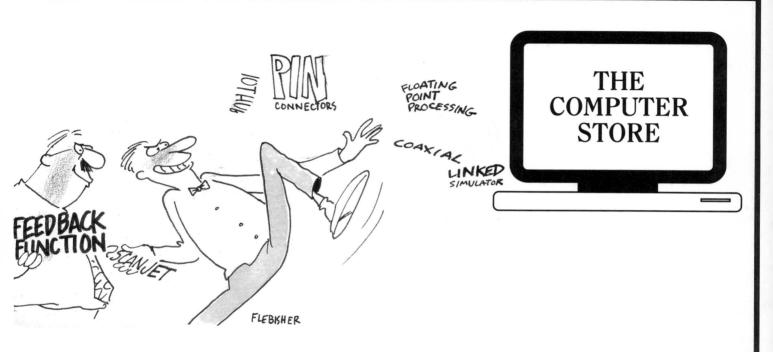

The salesperson will usually win these acronym-hurling contests because they've been better trained, and will send the customer off with their purchase and a promise of endless support to help solve whatever problems arise. This is true only until your check clears or until they leave to become a used-car salesman.

HONEYMOONING WITH A COMPUTER

*Leonard realized that he'd need
a bit more time than he had planned
to read his manuals.*

The honeymoon is the period just after marrying the computer when you have this good feeling that this electronic marvel will soon be solving all your problems. The honeymoon starts when you get the spiffy looking box home and lasts until you try to operate it yourself by reading the manuals.

HONEYMOONING
WITH A
COMPUTER

Herbert knew the honeymoon was over when his friend who loaded all the programs left and all he could get on his screen was INVALID COMMAND.

CONSUMMATING YOUR MARRIAGE

*Phil couldn't believe at how securely
his computer was packaged.*

You consummate a marriage to a computer when you open the box and take out all those odd shaped foam inserts that have been protecting your computer's virginity. If there are any of those plastic foam peanuts they will stick to everything in the room except the garbage can. You are supposed to save all the packing materials in case you ever have to ship your computer back for service, but since you'll never figure out how to correctly put it back together, just forget about it. Virginity is pretty tough to restore anyway.

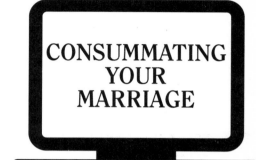

The second step in consummating a marriage to a computer is loading all the copyrighted programs you borrow from a friend. The FBI is constantly on the watch for people like you and it's best to do the pirating with the shades down. No one, it seems, ever BUYS programs themselves and it makes you wonder how all those software companies stay in business, not to mention having their stocks sell at these incredible multiples.

BEING MARRIED TO A COMPUTER CAN ROT YOUR BRAINS

Most people think computers rot your brains by doing the calculations you used to use your head to figure out. This may be true, but computers really do their damage by:

1. Providing an overload of information in the form of reports.
2. They do this on a monthly, or even more frequent, basis.
3. Because it's from a computer, the information appears to be accurate so you believe it.
4. The information has just enough totally stupid errors in it to render it completely useless.

MEALTIMES
WITH YOUR
COMPUTER

Truly advanced computers are indistinguishable from coke machines.

"Honey, I think she's learning to use it."

WHAT ABOUT THE UNFAITHFUL COMPUTER?

An unfaithful computer lets other people see your information, lets other people play with it, picks up viruses and other diseases all over the place. The only solution, if you find your computer is unfaithful, is to sell it for a small fraction of its original cost and get another. Wayward computers can seldom be trusted and if you can't believe your computer, you will never have any confidence in its output.

COMPUTER COMMANDS YOU'D BETTER RESPECT

1. Do you really want to delete this file?
2. Report about to be printed requires 25,000 sheets of paper.
3. Format your hard drive.

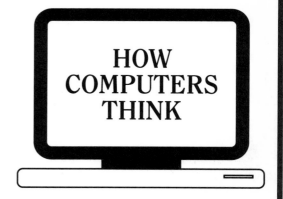

HOW COMPUTERS THINK

As everyone knows, computers think by turning little switches on and off. This seems pretty silly but since computers can turn these little switches on and off very quickly, sort of like a 3-year-old playing with the first light switch he can reach, they can annoy the electrons into doing arithmetic. This doesn't happen with our average 3-year-old because they annoy their parents long before they get to the electrons.

How Bugs Really Get Into Your Computer

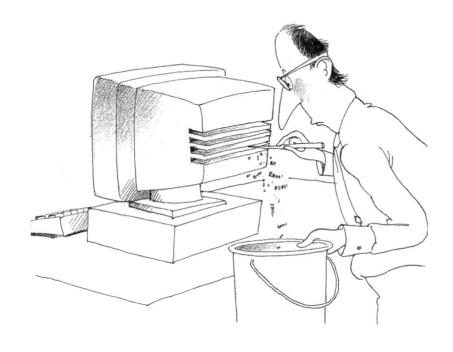

Where Garbled Commands Really End Up

TRAVELING WITH YOUR COMPUTER

Marvin noticed that many of his fellow travelers had computers much more compact than his.

A fat computer isn't as good a travel companion as a skinny model. Besides the weight and unmanageability, you will have to contend with people on the plane snickering at your full figured mate, while they sit proudly alongside their thin associate. Once a man got on a TWA flight with a fat computer and the person they now call the flight attendant (but who is really, as any intelligent person knows, the stewardess), had to give him a seat belt extension to secure it to the middle seat. He was so embarrassed that he spent the rest of the flight in the toilet.

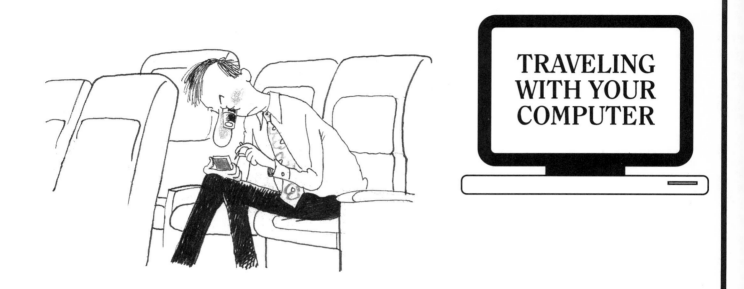

So you'll probably need a special traveling computer, and the smaller the better. The so called Laptop and Notebook computers become more prestigious as they get smaller in size. Some of the best and most expensive beauties are so small that they become absolutely useless for any operation that involves seeing or touching.

WHY COMPUTER MARRIAGES ARE SO DEMANDING

When writing programs, the first 90% of the projects take 90% of the time.
The remaining 10% takes about four times longer.

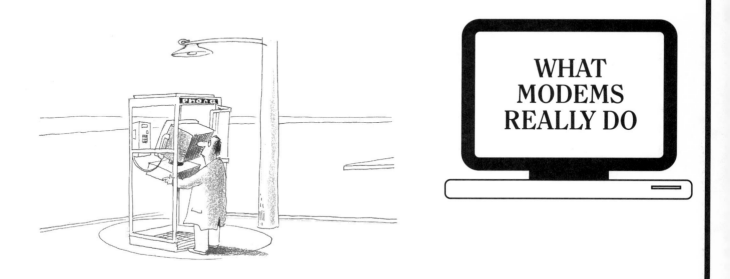

Successful marriages are based on good communication. A communicating computer is a happy computer. Modems enable computers to talk to one another. Computers need to talk to one another because they are lonely. They're lonely because computers are, underneath their incredible arithmetic efficiency, basically unbelievably stupid creatures. Have you ever talked to a computer? I certainly hope not.

HOW TO TELL IF YOU'VE MARRIED A FAT COMPUTER

1. You have 140 Munga bytes of memory.
2. It's all filled.
3. You have separate hard disk storage.
4. It's all filled.
5. It takes all weekend to retrieve any information.
6. It keeps begging for more.

HOW TO PUT YOUR COMPUTER ON A DIET

1. Throw out your sounds.
2. Delete the 97 Sim City Games you intended to finish someday.
3. Purge the X-rated screen savers you're too embarrassed to use.

"But Mr. Finkelstein, everyone knows data expands to fill the hard disks available."

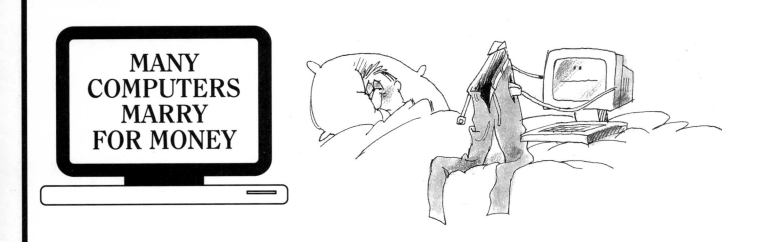

I know it's hard to believe, but many computers will marry for your money. You've found a super new 486 or 386 chip computer with gargantuan memory, and quadrupled MHz speed and it's discounted down to a tenth the original price, plus you get $9,000.00 worth of free software and a T-shirt, plus a library of manuals that will force you to build a new addition on your house. Not to mention a warranty good until 15 minutes before the machine crashes totally. So, of course, you come up with the pittance that is the purchase price, little realizing that this is just the beginning...

Shortly after you get this beauty home you find you need another hard disk drive, a few additional fonts, add-on boards, a modem, some vague interface, 9 function remote control track ball and a 117 pin adapter cord you can't fully understand what to hook the thing up to, to do anything useful—and this is only the first day!

"If carpenters built buildings the way programmers write programs,
then civilization would be destroyed by the first woodpecker to come along."

**KEEPING
YOUR
COMPUTER
HEALTHY**

Computers like:
1. Surge protectors.
2. Dust Covers.
3. Operators who wash their hands after eating melted chocolate.
4. Sweet nothings and encouraging words when starting up after a long, hard winter.

KEEPING YOUR COMPUTER HEALTHY

Computers hate:
1. People poking boards in their insides.
2. Coke or coffee spills on their keyboard.
3. Long bumpy trips in the trunk of cars.
4. Peanut butter smears on their floppy disks.
5. Operators who haven't showered in days.

Everyone realizes that computer viruses are created by diabolical programming weirdos who derive intense joy from generating mischief with people's time. Thankfully, there are plenty of programs around to purge these viruses, which are probably written by exactly the same kind of person. It's like buying medicine from a bacteria.

TAKING YOUR COMPUTER FOR GRANTED

When you start to take your computer for granted, that's when your hot romance starts to bite the dust. As soon as you become confident about your relationship, you are in mortal danger of erasing everything you've ever stored. The danger signs are:

1. You don't buy your computer sweet presents.
2. You don't back-up everything.
3. You become very intolerant of errors.

HOW TO TELL IF YOU'VE MARRIED A DULL COMPUTER

1. It doesn't play games with you.
2. It doesn't communicate well and hardly listens.
3. It's refused access to your favorite bulletin boards.

Every office has a person who understands computers and can help you with the different problems that are sure to arise. Seek this person out and make friends with him.

This is always a painful and unpleasant task. Divorcing a computer means you have to:

1. Transfer its data to a format that will be totally incompatible with your present one.
2. Learn new operating systems.

Besides, if there are children such as modems, hard drives, etc., they will be incompatible with your new computer and the divorce becomes even more expensive.

"That new Apple is as user friendly as they come."

BAD THINGS TO SAY TO YOUR COMPUTER

1. This looks easy.
2. There should be plenty of memory.
3. I need this by 2 p.m.
4. I sure don't want to lose this data.
5. I'll just leave you to print this out.

GOOD THINGS TO SAY TO YOUR COMPUTER

1. I think I'll buy more memory.
2. I'll just stay here and watch you calculate.
3. I guess I'll renew the service policy.
4. I'm going to get an entire dedicated power station for this computer.
5. Now that I've won the lottery, I think I'll spend all that money on upgrades.

"This multi media is terrific. Now when I open my printouts I have a pornographic picture on every page and it plays Beethoven's 5th."

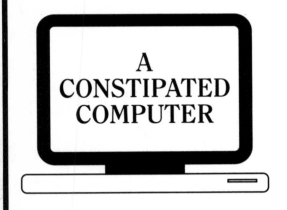

A
CONSTIPATED
COMPUTER

Sometimes your computer will get sluggish. It acts as though it is all stuffed up, moving slowly and listlessly. It has a vague feeling of wanting to move but has only a disappointing ability to do so. You have a constipated computer. Any grunts or unfamiliar moans are major clues.

*Besides being constipated, Vinnie found
computers moody and unstable at certain
times of the month.*

A
CONSTIPATED
COMPUTER

There are a few ways to loosen up a constipated computer. (Are you ready?
It's a hands-on job.)
1. Purges and diets are quick but painful solutions.
2. More memory may help.
3. Sometimes a new program can release the pressure.
4. In severe cases, you may have to seek divorce and get a bigger computer.

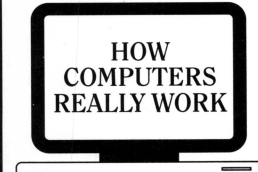

HOW COMPUTERS REALLY WORK

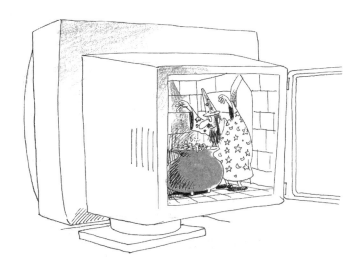

No one really knows how they REALLY work. Well, maybe my nephew David at M.I.T., but almost no one else. I mean everyone knows basic binary systems and chips, and on and off, but how does all this print out spread sheets, or play interplanetary attack games? Any sufficiently advanced technology is indiscernible from magic, so you might as well figure computers work on magic and be done with it.

LAWS
OF
PROGRAMMING

1. A smoothly running program is probably obsolete.
2. Any useful program will have to be updated.
3. Any given program costs more and takes longer.
4. It is better to start over than to transfer information from one system to another.
5. Any given program will expand to fill all available memory.

Someone programmed Sylvia's computer to celebrate her birthday
with a major multi-media extravaganza.

Dean decided to spring for a computer work station the third time he spilled coffee on his keyboard.

KEEPING THE MAGIC IN YOUR MARRIAGE

"Any sufficiently advanced technology is indistinguishable from magic."
The magic may go out of your marriage if you become too familiar with your computer. Look into the innards of a computer, figure out how it works and you are liable to realize you're married to a shallow, stupid and worst of all, ungrateful dork. After all, computers have simple minds albeit with this ability to do simple things very quickly.

KEEPING THE MAGIC IN YOUR MARRIAGE

"Well, is this trial separation working?"

Some ways to keep the magic going in your relationship are to:
1. Find new games you can play together.
2. Occasionally get away from each other, separate vacations for example.
3. Give yourself space to grow and learn individually.
4. Hook up with new systems.
5. Swap computers with good friends whose health records you're sure of.

GETTING SEPARATIONS FROM OLD COMPUTERS

Don't ever try to sell an old computer because it will only break your heart. Better, give it to a cousin or let the kids play with it out in the backyard. That electronic whiz that cost about $2,000,000 and came with a bevy of handlers and salesmen in a bullet-proof shipping container will now cost a $60 "environmental charge" if you want it hauled away.

MAKING MONEY WITH YOUR COMPUTER

A few people may make money by manufacturing hardware and writing software but the real money in computers is in teaching other people how to use one. It's sort of like a pyramid scheme where there is always another sucker willing to spend money to learn how to operate a computer. The scheme should collapse once everyone knows how to use their machines and the 9 million experts are all trying to teach the remaining 7 grandmothers how to sort their recipes.

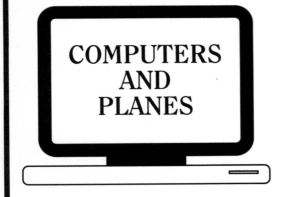

COMPUTERS AND PLANES

I've never sat next to anyone on a plane that didn't work for a computer company. I mean these people must travel constantly. "And what do you do?" "Oh, I'm in system design" or "computer analysis" or "software development." And it must be even worse up in first class, but I wouldn't know.

Need to store the names and sexual preferences of everyone in the world? How about adding every book printed since the Gütenberg Bible to your lap top? No problem—just buy, for a little more than a case of beer, a hard disk drive with 60 trillion trigabytes of storage. And then tell me computers don't work by magic.

It's important to teach your cleaning people never to towel your computer. More marriages have been wrecked by these people than you'd ever believe.

A good marriage partner knows when it's time to take a break.

COMPUTER BOXES

Computers come packed in the most clever shipping cartons. When you open these ingenious boxes, you know it would take a nuclear detonation to disturb the contents. The problem then arises as to where to store these monuments of foam padding and stiff fiber inserts. I mean in case you ever want to ship a computer back, you need the box, or the warranty will be voided. So you stick the box in your attic or cellar, plus a similar box for every accessory, and if you're like me, you create a fire hazard in your storage area the size of Montana.

WHERE COMPUTERS ARE MADE

The inner, inner really magic parts of a computer are all made in a little known Asian country by carefully trained teenagers. These kids become really nimble with their fingers by snacking on slippery pine nuts with chopsticks. I'm not making this up. Better to have these kids making computer innards than out smashing mailboxes or experimenting with back seat sex like our teenagers.

PRIVACY
AND YOUR
COMPUTER

PERSONAL
COMPUTERS
TELL ALL
TODAY
ON...OPRAH!

Your computer knows all your private information, all your secrets and probably
most of your indiscretions. Lots of people, not to mention the IRS, would love to
learn these secrets, but you of course have these well protected with codes and
passwords. Would you sleep less easy tonight knowing that $29 programs are
available to unlock these codes in about 12 seconds? Hell, these people can get into
top secret military computers that control bombs! Your security is a big, fat <u>bad</u> joke.
When you forget your password, you'll be happy to use these code breakers yourself.

Joey and his fellow hackers manage to break into the regional drug dealers' customer list.

"Adam's playing with his new magnet kit."

"Honey, did you bother with a backup this morning?"

When a computer thinks the information you are working with is really important, it says, " Hey, let's have some fun with this person" and the probability of a crash goes way up. Sophisticated operators will always try to convince the computer that the work they're doing is trivial.

WHEN YOUR COMPUTER WANTS <u>YOU</u> TO LOSE WEIGHT

Sometimes your computer will start pestering you to lose weight. "Hey", the computer says, "you've been purging me all the time...how about you getting rid of some of that cellulite that jiggles whenever you punch my keyboard?" You've got to nip this kind of attitude in the bud or you'll find your whole life controlled by the stupid bugger. If your machine gets insistent, roll up a user manual and smash it on its function board.

PLEASE HELP
MY COMPUTER
NEEDS MORE
MEMORY

"Marcia insists on scanning each of her dates into her diary."

HOW TRIVIAL INFORMATION IS DELETED

You:	Delete this file
Computer:	Do you really want to delete this file?
You:	Yes
Computer:	Type yes three times
You:	Yes Yes Yes
Computer:	What's your grandmother's maiden name?
You:	Von Bletsky
Computer:	Last chance to cancel deletion. Are you sure?
You:	Dammit, YES!
Computer:	Cross your heart?

HOW REALLY
IMPORTANT
INFORMATION
IS DELETED

The People Who Name Computer Components

"That laser jet printer just has a mind of its own."

COMPUTER MANUALS

Once there was a hacker named Henry who lived in Nebraska and understood computer manuals. Henry was a high school drop-out who started building computers from bent paper clips and later, was able to break into secret Pentagon computers and start brush fire wars with impunity. Anyhow, no one since then has really understood computer manuals and if you're smart, you'll only buy programs your friends already have and can explain to you (As long as you're doing that you might as well save some money and copy the program but DON'T COPY THIS BOOK.).

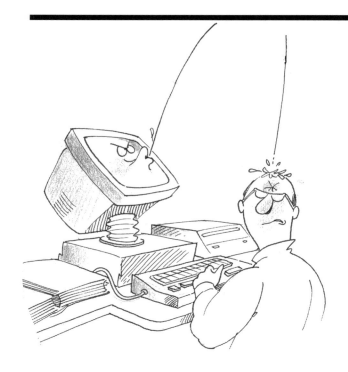

USER UNFRIENDLY ERROR MESSAGES

Just Exactly What Do You Mean?
You're an Asshole.
How Stupid Can You Get?
What Kind of Dumb Command is That?

LAP TOPS AND PALM TOPS

These incredibly compact computers enable businessmen and women to take their friends' addresses and all sorts of computer games along on trips, and then they're able to play these games on planes, in hotels and in bathrooms. Once a skier named Dean tried to do some actual work on his portable computer at a ski lodge, but he was ostracized by all his friends until he returned to playing solitaire.

PHONING
FOR
HELP

You have a problem with some program or a piece of hardware so you dial the 800 number for help. After you've been beep-beeped around a little and you've used your touch-tone phone to spell out the equivalent of the Gettysburg Address, perhaps you'll be lucky enough to speak to a real person. This person is an expert, a guru, who can easily solve problems such as the one you're facing. He or she will be happy to do so but just to convince you of their superiority, they will bury you in so much technical information that your own problem will appear to be trivial and you'll find yourself saying "yes, yes" just to get off the phone as quickly as you can.

Ask a programmer if the machine can provide some specific new information. They will first list about a thousand things they can give you right away. Next, they will patiently explain that with a little effort they can format the information into another thousand ways, none of which are quite what you want. Finally, they will admit they can do it but that it'll be faster if you did it by hand.

ANSWERS FROM YOUR PROGRAMMER

1. It's already in the system.
2. It'll take more storage space than you have.
3. Someone has already done it but we can't find it.
4. There'll be a new program for that on the market in a few months.
5. I'll think it over (they don't know).

Static electricity on the new large screen work station
delays Kathy's lunch.

It's very true. A user-friendly computer is like a comfortable old shoe,
or a pair of pants that don't itch or a marriage made in heaven.

POWER FROM YOUR MARRIAGE

"Leonardo – no one's gong to respect that handwritten stuff."

Marrying a computer gives you a certain power. Computer print-outs and screens have a definite believability that inspires confidence and trust, especially among the computer ignorant masses. Computers let you forcefully present your ideas in a format that people are afraid to question. These poor ignoramuses don't realize computers can lie, cheat and fudge much better than humans.

If you leave the room (or sometimes even look away) when a printer is printing, one of the following will happen:
1. It'll run out of paper.
2. The paper will jam.
3. It will compress your entire report onto one line.

Password – a secret code that is forgotten almost immediately after it is installed

Spellcheck – an incredible system that proves just how ridiculous your 3rd grade teacher's priorities were

State of Art – a very brief moment in time between your purchase of a computer and the improved model's introduction at a lower price

COMPUTER
DEFINITIONS

New Version — a modern system for introducing viruses and bugs into your computer

On Line Help — a system for taking up memory with instructions you can't use

Font — name of an insidious style of letters conceived by software companies to entice users to buy so their literature can look like 18th century ads

An impeccably formatted presentation can fool 100% of the people 100% of the time.

Thank you for calling Software World. Your call is important to us, so please stay on the line. "Beep"

Computer nerds go to a screen-saver party.

The Future of Computers